What's In Your Hand? Ex. 4:2
Career Guidance

Interactive Self-Assessment Tools
for
Career Evaluation & Implementation

Are you trying to figure out what career you want?

Have you recently been laid off or terminated?

Are you thinking about changing careers?

If you answered "yes" to any of these questions, this interactive guide can help you get started toward a satisfying and fulfilling career.

In researching and putting this guide together, many thanks go to my friends and family who were so gracious to give me their feedback. Special thanks go to my husband Gary for his suggestions and encouragement and to my son Chris for his time, advice, and critique.

What's In Your Hand? Ex. 4:2
Career Guidance

Introduction

The title of this interactive career guide is in reference to the encounter Moses had at the burning bush. God used the transformation of the staff in Moses' hand to assure Moses that He would be with him and equip him to complete the work God had for him to do. I believe God has a place where He wants His children to serve/witness for Him and will equip them for the task, as He did Moses, to accomplish His work in the world (see page 25 annotation). How has God equipped you to fulfill His purpose for your life? What's in your hand?

Perhaps you are searching for a career, have been laid off or terminated, or are thinking of changing careers. You might be confused about which direction to go and how to get started, disorganized and frustrated in your approach, or in need of validation and encouragement.

This interactive career guide is comprehensive, quick, concise, organized, and easy-to-understand. It is designed so that you can go through it individually or with a small group. The first portion (evaluation) takes a broad look at all the essential factors for career selection and then helps you narrow down and tie it altogether into a concise and comprehensive career goal. The second portion (implementation) provides tools to help you pursue and obtain your ideal career. The last portion (addendum) contains additional aids to assist you.

Table of Contents

Evaluation →

In the first portion of this interactive guide, you'll assess and determine essential factors (listed below) for selecting a satisfying career. As you proceed, you'll be making choices in each area. You'll start with a broad spectrum in each area and, as you progress, you'll narrow down your choices until finally you have a concise career goal. This first portion may affirm your career choice or lead you into another realm of possibility.

<u>In Preparation:</u>

Interests/Transferable Skills +
Values + Location + Environment +
People + Tools + Information +
Responsibility + Supervision +
Compensation + Benefits =

Ideal Career Goal

<u>LET'S GET STARTED!</u>

What's In Your Hand? Ex. 4:2

Career Guidance

Interests/Transferable Skills

In choosing a career, it's important to consider one that utilizes the interests and transferable skills God has given you. Transferable skills are those that can be transferred to any chosen career.

To begin, look over the list of interests/transferable skills on this page and the next. Note: this is not an exhaustive list. There is room on page 3 to fill in other interests/transferable skills that you consider important and that apply to you.

Now, check off the words that answer the following questions:

1) How do you like to spend your time? (first square in the columns below)
2) What have others said you are good at doing? (second square in the columns below)
3) What words describe your accomplishments? (third square in the columns below)

□ □ □ account	□ □ □ construct	□ □ □ enforce
□ □ □ acquire/collect	□ □ □ consult	□ □ □ engineer
□ □ □ administrate	□ □ □ control	□ □ □ enlighten
□ □ □ advise	□ □ □ convert	□ □ □ enter data
□ □ □ analyze	□ □ □ coordinate	□ □ □ entertain/host
□ □ □ arbitrate	□ □ □ counsel/coach	□ □ □ estimate
□ □ □ arrange/sort	□ □ □ craft	□ □ □ evaluate
□ □ □ assemble	□ □ □ critique	□ □ □ examine
□ □ □ assess	□ □ □ cure/treat	□ □ □ exercise
□ □ □ assist	□ □ □ decorate	□ □ □ experiment
□ □ □ audit	□ □ □ delegate	□ □ □ facilitate
□ □ □ beautify	□ □ □ deliver	□ □ □ find patterns
□ □ □ calculate	□ □ □ design	□ □ □ forecast
□ □ □ campaign	□ □ □ detect/identify	□ □ □ formulate
□ □ □ catalog/categorize	□ □ □ develop	□ □ □ guide/nurture
□ □ □ classify	□ □ □ diagnose	□ □ □ handle
□ □ □ collaborate/confer	□ □ □ discover	□ □ □ imagine
□ □ □ compare	□ □ □ dispense/distribute	□ □ □ implement
□ □ □ compile	□ □ □ display	□ □ □ improve
□ □ □ compose	□ □ □ dissect	□ □ □ inform/explain
□ □ □ compute	□ □ □ draft	□ □ □ initiate
□ □ □ conceive	□ □ □ dramatize/act	□ □ □ innovate/create
□ □ □ conceptualize	□ □ □ draw	□ □ □ inspect
□ □ □ conduct	□ □ □ edit	□ □ □ inspire
□ □ □ consolidate	□ □ □ encourage/empower	□ □ □ install

Interests/Transferable Skills (continued)

1) How do you like to spend your time? (first square in the columns below)
2) What have others said you are good at doing? (second square in the columns below)
3) What words describe your accomplishments? (third square in the columns below)

☐ ☐ ☐ institute	☐ ☐ ☐ perform	☐ ☐ ☐ serve
☐ ☐ ☐ integrate	☐ ☐ ☐ photograph	☐ ☐ ☐ set up
☐ ☐ ☐ interpret	☐ ☐ ☐ plan	☐ ☐ ☐ sew
☐ ☐ ☐ invent	☐ ☐ ☐ plant	☐ ☐ ☐ shape
☐ ☐ ☐ inventory	☐ ☐ ☐ predict	☐ ☐ ☐ sketch/illustrate
☐ ☐ ☐ invest	☐ ☐ ☐ prepare	☐ ☐ ☐ solve
☐ ☐ ☐ lead/direct	☐ ☐ ☐ prescribe	☐ ☐ ☐ streamline
☐ ☐ ☐ liaison	☐ ☐ ☐ process	☐ ☐ ☐ structure
☐ ☐ ☐ locate	☐ ☐ ☐ produce	☐ ☐ ☐ style/fashion
☐ ☐ ☐ maintain	☐ ☐ ☐ program	☐ ☐ ☐ supervise
☐ ☐ ☐ make decisions	☐ ☐ ☐ promote/present	☐ ☐ ☐ supply
☐ ☐ ☐ manage	☐ ☐ ☐ protect	☐ ☐ ☐ support
☐ ☐ ☐ manufacture	☐ ☐ ☐ record	☐ ☐ ☐ survey
☐ ☐ ☐ market	☐ ☐ ☐ recruit	☐ ☐ ☐ synthesize
☐ ☐ ☐ mediate	☐ ☐ ☐ regulate	☐ ☐ ☐ tailor
☐ ☐ ☐ mentor	☐ ☐ ☐ rehabilitate	☐ ☐ ☐ teach/train
☐ ☐ ☐ model	☐ ☐ ☐ repair/fix	☐ ☐ ☐ tend
☐ ☐ ☐ monitor/track	☐ ☐ ☐ report	☐ ☐ ☐ transcribe
☐ ☐ ☐ motivate	☐ ☐ ☐ represent/advocate	☐ ☐ ☐ translate
☐ ☐ ☐ navigate	☐ ☐ ☐ research	☐ ☐ ☐ troubleshoot
☐ ☐ ☐ negotiate	☐ ☐ ☐ restore	☐ ☐ ☐ verify
☐ ☐ ☐ observe	☐ ☐ ☐ retrieve	☐ ☐ ☐ write
☐ ☐ ☐ operate	☐ ☐ ☐ screen	☐ ☐ ☐ _____
☐ ☐ ☐ organize	☐ ☐ ☐ sculpt	☐ ☐ ☐ _____
☐ ☐ ☐ paint	☐ ☐ ☐ sell/persuade	☐ ☐ ☐ _____

When finished with these two pages, highlight those words with three checks so they stand out.

Now thoughtfully consider the interests/skills you've just highlighted and select <u>at least four</u> but <u>no more than seven</u> to transfer to page 8.

What meaning/context do you attach to each of the interests/skills you've selected?

_____

_____

_____

_____

_____

Career Guidance

Values

Now consider a career that aligns with your values. Your values are the passions that energize you and give your daily activities meaning. Look over the list of values on this page. Note: this is not an exhaustive list. There is room at the bottom to fill in other values that you consider important and that apply to you.

Select words from the list below that answer these three questions:

1) What words describe what's important to you; what gets you fired up? (square one)
2) What have others said you are passionate about? (square two)
3) What issues/situations have you worked through where you felt satisfaction? (square three)

□ □ □ Accuracy   □ □ □ Achievement   □ □ □ Application   □ □ □ Artistry

□ □ □ Community   □ □ □ Connections   □ □ □ Creativity   □ □ □ Cultural Diversity

□ □ □ Development   □ □ □ Discipline   □ □ □ Education   □ □ □ Efficiency

□ □ □ Excellence   □ □ □ Family   □ □ □ Finances   □ □ □ Freedom

□ □ □ Friendship   □ □ □ Government   □ □ □ Health/Fitness   □ □ □ Hospitality

□ □ □ Independence   □ □ □ Individualism   □ □ □ Influence   □ □ □ Intellect

□ □ □ Justice   □ □ □ Lawfulness   □ □ □ Leadership   □ □ □ Loyalty

□ □ □ Mentoring   □ □ □ Ministry   □ □ □ Music   □ □ □ Opportunity

□ □ □ Performance   □ □ □ Preparedness   □ □ □ Product   □ □ □ Productivity

□ □ □ Poverty   □ □ □ Professionalism   □ □ □ Rapport   □ □ □ Reputation

□ □ □ Security   □ □ □ Service   □ □ □ Social Correctness □ □ □ Solutions

□ □ □ Sports   □ □ □ Structure   □ □ □ Teamwork   □ □ □ Tolerance

□ □ □ _____   □ □ □ _____   □ □ □ _____   □ □ □ _____

When finished, from those with three checks, select <u>at least four</u> but <u>no more than seven</u> to transfer to page 8.

In what ways do you see these values motivating you in your career? _____

_____

_____

_____

What's In Your Hand? Ex. 4:2
Career Guidance

Location & Environment

Have you thought about where you would like to work? Location and environment are important considerations in choosing a career.

Location:

Envision and describe the physical location in which you would like to work. Here are a few ideas to get you thinking. Transfer your responses to page 8. Note: this is not an exhaustive list.

Circle the location that appeals to you or enter another option. Do you want to work...

    ...in a church?   ...in a high-rise?   ...in a hospital?

    ...in an industrial complex? ...in a lab?   ....in an office?

    ...outdoors?   ...in a police or fire station? ...in a restaurant?

    ...in a school?   ...in a store?   ...in a studio?

    ...or _____

Do you want to work from home? _____

Do you want a career that requires you to travel? _____

How far are you willing to commute to and from work? _____

Environment:

Envision and describe the environment in which you would like to work. Here are a few ideas to get you thinking. Transfer your responses to page 8. Note: this is not an exhaustive list.

Circle the environment(s) that appeals to you or enter another option. Do you want to work in an environment that is...

    ...academic?   ...busy?   ...casual?

    ...challenging?   ...dynamic?   ...fun?

    ...goal-oriented?   ...hectic?   ...non-traditional?

    ...orderly?   ...professional?   ...routine?

    ...slow-paced?   ...spiritual?   ...technical?

    ...or _____

What's In Your Hand? Ex. 4:2

Career Guidance

People, Tools & Information

Now consider the people, tools and information that are in the location and environment you've selected. Answer the following questions on this page and then transfer your responses to page 8. Envision and describe the following in your ideal career:

Who are the **people** you are working with throughout the day?
(For example: children, tourists, infants, customers, teens, athletes, Christians, injured, underprivileged, seniors, agents, politicians)

_____

_____

Are these people the main focus of your work or do they support the main focus of your work? _____

_____

What **tools/equipment/materials** are you using throughout the day?
(For example: surgical, kitchen, building, office, Scripture/study, navigational, manufacturing, automotive, artistic, theatrical, photography, agricultural)

_____

_____

Are these tools/equipment/materials the main focus of your work or do they support the main focus of your work? _____

_____

What **information** are you working with throughout the day?
(For example: scientific data, curriculum, weather, regulations, Biblical truth, archives, movies/plays, fashion trends, medical reports, sports facts, numbers, strategies)

_____

_____

Is this information the main focus of your work or does it support the main focus of your work? _____

_____

Responsibility, Supervision, Compensation & Benefits

What type of **responsibility** do you want in a career? Select one of the following or give an alternative. Transfer your response to page 8. Note: this is not an exhaustive list.

Do you prefer a career that…

☐ …allows you to define the position?
What would that look like? _____
_____

☐ …is loosely defined and allows you to operate independently?
What would that look like? _____
_____

☐ …is defined but allows you the flexibility to create and grow within it?
What would that look like? _____
_____

☐ …is specifically defined but allows you a little flexibility?
What would that look like? _____
_____

☐ …is specific and requires that you fulfill it as defined?
What would that look like? _____
_____

☐ …or _____
What would that look like? _____
_____

Answer the following questions and transfer your responses to page 8.

What type of **supervision** do you prefer?
_____

How much **compensation** do you need?
_____

What type of **benefits** do you need?
_____

Career Guidance

Essential Factors for Career Evaluation/Selection

| Interests/Transferable Skills | Values |

| Location | Environment |

| People | Tools |

| Information | Responsibility |

| Supervision | Compensation & Benefits |

As you look over your selections, what pattern do you see? What ideal career are you starting to picture? _____

_____

_____

_____

What's In Your Hand? Ex. 4:2
Career Guidance

Self-Assessment & Career Goal

Let's tie everything together! Using the essential factors you listed on page 8, answer the questions below to help you identify your career goal. Relax and picture a day in your ideal career (the one you'll feel guilty getting paid for).

1. How are you using your interests/skills in the career you're picturing?

   _____.

2. How does the career align with your values?

   _____.

3. How important is the location and what role does the environment play?

   _____.

4. How do the people fit into your career? How are you interacting with them?

   _____.

5. What role do the tools have and how are you using the information?

   _____.

6. How much responsibility do you have?

   _____.

7. What type of supervision do you have and how important is that?

   _____.

8. What ideal compensation and benefits package meets your needs/wants?

   _____.

9. What is the career you're picturing? (See page 11 for help, if needed.)

   _____.

Now write your own career goal. (See sample career goals on page 10.)

_____

_____

_____

_____

Sample Career Goals

Here are six career goals, two of which are broken down for you. Refer to these samples in writing your own career goal on page 9.

A satisfying career is one in which I assist churches in showing excellence and accuracy in presentation by analyzing and editing promotional literature. As an editor, I use a computer at home and collaborate with two to three staff members at each church.

- Your preferred skills: analyzing, editing & collaborating
- Your preferred values: excellence and accuracy in presentation
- The location and environment in which you prefer to work: at home
- The kind of people you want to work with: church staff members
- The kind of tools/information you want to work with: computer & promotional literature

I want a career teaching a class of about thirty elementary-age children in a Christian school. It's important to me that children are influenced by the Word of God and its application on a daily basis. I also want to create new programs to help teach age-appropriate curriculum in a Christian setting.

- Your preferred skills: teaching & creating new programs
- Your preferred values: influence and application of the Word of God daily
- The location and environment in which you prefer to work: Christian school
- The kind of people you want to work with: elementary-age children
- The kind of tools/information you want to work with: Word of God & curriculum

A satisfying career is one in which I repair and maintain vehicles to keep them at peak performance. It's important to me that drivers and passengers are protected and that I have a good reputation as a mechanic for excellent work that brings in new business and keeps regular customers coming back. I want to work in a large automotive center as part of a dynamic team that provides high-quality service and offers adequate compensation.

Because I care about the health of others, I prefer a nursing career in which I treat severely-ill elderly people in an orderly-run hospice and maintain a detailed medical record of their progress for their doctors. The compensation and benefits would need to be negotiable.

Because I care about lawfulness and security, a satisfying career is one in which I protect and serve the public by monitoring the hectic streets of Los Angeles as a police officer. As a follow-up to my daily activities, I organize data and prepare reports.

A satisfying career is one in which I work as a corporate trainer for a goal-oriented organization located in a high-rise. I have a lot of responsibility, but I have a supervisor who gives me a lot of leeway. I confer with managers regarding the development of their staff and together we decide on and implement a plan of action for their employees.

Career Fields

If you have not yet decided on a career, this page is designed to help you think about various career fields and the many occupations within them. Choose a field(s) and then, as you research the field(s), fill in occupations that interest you. Note: this is not an exhaustive list.

Administration

Agriculture

Art

Business

Construction

Design

Education

Electronics

Engineering

Entertainment

Entrepreneurship

Finance

Fitness

Food

Government

Hospitality

Information

Law

Manufacturing

Marketing

Mechanics

Medicine

Military

Ministry

Music

Parachurch

Public Relations

Public Service

Real Estate

Retail

Science

Social Work

Sports

Technology

Tourism

Trade Craft

Training

Transportation

Writing

Other (   )

← **Evaluation**

The first half of this interactive guide was designed to help you assess and determine essential factors for selecting a satisfying career.

In Summary:

Interests/Transferable Skills +
Values + Location + Environment +
People + Tools + Information +
Responsibility + Supervision +
Compensation + Benefits =

Ideal Career Goal

Implementation →

The second half of this interactive guide provides tools to help you pursue and obtain that career.

In Succession:

Resume + Cover Letter +
Networking +
Information Interviewing +
Employment Interviewing =

Ideal Career Search

Resume Writing

Congratulations on completing a career goal! Before you begin purposefully sharing your goal with others (networking), you'll want to have a resume available to hand out. The purpose of a resume is to present your skills and accomplishments to a potential employer.

There are two basic types of resumes. While both emphasize skills and accomplishments, a **chronological** resume highlights time frames of employment while a **functional** resume deemphasizes them. There are samples on the next two pages.

Chronological resumes are usually written when there is a consistent work history and the writer wishes to point this out.

Functional resumes are usually written when there has been little to no previous employment, there is a gap in work history, or when experience rather than age of the applicant is the emphasis.

In general, resumes can be designed to match positions you are applying for so that an employer can readily line up and compare the skill set stated on your resume with what he/she wants done in the position.

Skills and accomplishments should constitute the bulk of your resume. To design accomplishment statements, state what benefits or results occurred and what you did to achieve them. Ask yourself such questions as: How did I…

…improve teamwork?	…make things easier?
…accomplish more with the same?	…solve a problem?
…create something new?	…overcome obstacles?
…establish a new procedure?	

Other inclusions should be where you've worked/volunteered, your education, credentials/certificates you hold, memberships, committees, and boards (as appropriate).

Resumes should be one page. They should be error-free and look attractive on the page so as to catch the eye of the reader. Numbers and percentages should be incorporated where appropriate and action words should be allowed to do their job. CAPITALIZATION, bullets •, **bold print**, *italic*, and underlining should be used for emphasis and esthetics.

Resumes can be submitted at an employment interview, sent after an employment interview, or sent, along with a cover letter (see page 16), to request an employment interview. At times resumes are required in order to be considered for an interview.

Resumes can also be sent at random, along with cover letters, to people/organizations in a cold-call approach. Even though this is widely done, it is probably the least effective.

Resumes can also be used by headhunters to do the searching for you.

Remember to keep track of all the resumes you send out so you can follow up with each one.

Sample Chronological Resume

Matthew J. Miller
4567 Regency St.
Somewhere, CA 11111
Phone/Email: _____

EMPLOYMENT HISTORY:

2012-Present **World Help International**   Marionville, CA
Educational Development Specialist
> Trained 30 international student development workers in a new procedure reducing the time required to process and transport students.

> Designed and implemented new evaluation programs that eliminated educational inequities that 7 third-world countries were experiencing.

> Increased efficiency by establishing a committee to review and revise agency policies and procedures effecting students in over 50 countries.

2005-2012 **Countries Abroad**   Newhall, SC
Analyst/Trainer
> Analyzed 500 individual educational profiles for transferable credits resulting in acceptance to U.S. colleges and universities for over 60%.

> Improved teamwork by training ten other interviewers/analysts to handle increasing numbers of foreign student profiles requesting transfers to U.S.

1995-2005 **Resettlement International**   Nashville, OR
Education Coordinator
> Developed and instituted more economical English-language educational programs for over 50 colleges and universities saving cost by 20%.

> Solved student resettlement processing problems by establishing new procedures with 70% success rate.

EDUCATION:
M.A.   International Communication   University of Utah
B.A.   Social Sciences   University of Miami

PUBLICATIONS:
Twenty articles for the U.S. Government Research Team   IEC Publications

BOARD MEMBERSHIPS:
Relief & Relocation Institute of America
United International Training Organization

Sample Functional Resume

Matthew J. Miller
4567 Regency St.
Somewhere, CA 11111
Phone/Email: _____

Career Highlights: Over 20 years international development & training

SKILLS & ACCOMPLISHMENTS:
- Trained 30 international student development workers in a new procedure reducing the time required to process and transport students.

- Designed and implemented new evaluation programs that eliminated educational inequities that 7 third-world countries were experiencing.

- Increased efficiency by establishing a committee to review and revise agency policies and procedures effecting students in over 50 countries.

- Analyzed 500 individual educational profiles for transferable credits resulting in acceptance to U.S. colleges and universities for over 60%.

- Improved teamwork by training ten other interviewers/analysts to handle increasing numbers of foreign student profiles requesting transfers to U.S.

- Developed and instituted more economical English-language educational programs for over 50 colleges and universities saving cost by 20%.

- Solved student resettlement processing problems by establishing new procedures with 70% success rate.

EMPLOYMENT SUMMARY:

World Help International	Educational Development Specialist	Marionville, CA
Countries Abroad	Analyst/Trainer	Newhall, SC
Resettlement International	Education Coordinator	Nashville, OR

EDUCATION:

M.A.	International Communication	University of Utah
B.A.	Social Sciences	University of Miami

PUBLICATIONS:

Articles for the U.S. Government Research Team	IEC Publications

BOARD MEMBERSHIPS:
Relief & Relocation Institute of America
United International Training Organization

Resume Worksheet

This page is designed for you to jot down all pertinent/relevant information for your resume. Use the samples on pages 13 and 14 as templates.

As you write your resume, consider skills used in the home, past/current accomplishments in the workplace, church and school activities, volunteer work you've done, community assistance you've provided, and contributions you've made as a member of boards/committees.

Skills (see page 8)　　　　　Accomplishments　　　　　Benefits/Results

_____

_____

_____

_____

_____

_____

_____

_____

_____

_____

_____

_____

_____

_____

Employment: _____

Education: _____

Volunteer Work: _____

Credentials/Certificates/Awards: _____

Memberships/Committees/Boards: _____

_____

References are available upon request

This is an optional statement that can be centered at the bottom of your resume. References are letters of recommendation you have requested from those who know your abilities and work ethics. It's recommended to have them available for potential employers who may ask.

Cover Letter

Next prepare a cover letter. The purpose of a cover letter, that accompanies your resume, is to introduce yourself and request an employment interview. Whether you want to work for a particular individual or a particular organization, the following points should be considered. There is a sample on the following page.

- Address your letter to the individual you want to work for or, in the case of an organization you want to work for, address the letter to the person who has the authority to hire you.

- Make a connection, if possible, with someone you both know or someone who recommended you. This will help you stand out from other applicants.

- Focus on strengths you have that will best help meet their needs.

- Sell yourself by using action words and showing accomplishments that will get attention.

- See your cover letter from the vantage point of the reader. Consider what he/she might be looking for.

- Be brief and to the point.

Now consider…

To whom will you send a cover letter and resume? _____

_____

Who will your connection be? _____

If applying for a specific position, what is it? _____

Which skills, accomplishments, and benefits/results from your resume will you highlight in your cover letter? _____

_____

_____

_____

Sample Cover Letter

November 27, 20__

Matthew J. Miller
4567 Regency St.
Somewhere, CA 11111

Mr. Jeff Sample, Director of Administrative Services
Mission Advantage International
P.O. Box 7654
Anywhere, CA 00000

Dear Mr. Sample:

I was informed by Sarah Smith that you just had a student relocation position come open in your educational development department and were looking for someone with third-world country student relocation expertise.

I have worked in the area of international education over the last twenty years which included analyzing 500 individual educational profiles resulting in 60% acceptance to U.S. institutions. I have also solved student resettlement issues with a 70% success rate.

In addition, I have just submitted a fourth article, published through IEC (International Educators Consortium) Publications, on the advantages of designing evaluation programs in advance for third-world students.

I hope to discuss with you how my accomplishments in these areas might benefit your organization. I will call next week to discuss this possibility with you. Attached is a resume for your review.

Thank you for your time and consideration.

Sincerely,

(Signature)

Matthew J. Miller

Networking

Now that you have a career goal, resume, and cover letter completed, you can start purposefully networking. The end result of networking is to obtain names of people/organizations you'd like to research and perhaps work for.

It has been said that you are only one person away from the position you really want. The challenge is getting to that one person who can help you. To get the networking process started, make a list of everyone you know.

Friends/Family/Acquaintances/Casual Contacts/Professionals/Board Members/...

_____

_____

_____

_____

Explain to your contacts what type of career you're looking for. Ask them for names of people and organizations that are in your field of interest. Also ask if you may use their name as a reference. As your contacts give you possible people/organizations to contact, separate them into two categories: possible information interviews or possible employment interviews. The purpose of an information interview is designed solely to gain information (see page 19); the purpose of an employment interview is to procure a position (see page 20).

People/Organizations

Possible Information Interviews	Possible Employment Interviews
_____	_____
_____	_____
_____	_____
_____	_____
_____	_____
_____	_____

When finished with this page, make copies of the Interview Tracking Sheet (see page 22) or transfer the information onto file cards. Check off whether the purpose for each contact is an information interview or an employment interview. As you start making contact with the people/organizations, fill in the rest of the information as you proceed.

Information Interviewing

Once your possible-information-interview list is complete, identifying the people who can tell you the realities of the profession you're interested in, you're ready to set up information interviews. The purpose of an information interview is to obtain information from an individual in a particular career. You want to learn about the field to help you make a decision as to whether it's one you would enjoy.

What career fields interest you? _____

_____

What names have you been given or whom do you know in these fields?

_____

_____

Schedule an information interview appointment for about 20 minutes at a location of the individual's choice. To schedule the appointment, say something like: *"I am interested in gathering information about _____ career field. Would you have a few minutes to talk to me and give me some advice?"*

When you meet, ask the individual if he/she would mind if you took a few notes. After the interview, send a thank you note expressing appreciation for his/her time and insight. Make notes on your interview tracking sheet. If you are going through this material with a small group, pair off and practice information interviewing.

The most important question to ask is:

In the position you now hold, what does a typical day look like?

Other general questions you might ask:

How did you get into this career?

What are the most interesting aspects of your career?

What part of your career do you consider tedious or repetitious?

What are the prerequisites for a career in this field?

What other types of positions are available in this career field?

What is the current demand for individuals in this field?

How do you see this field changing over the next few years?

Who else would you suggest I talk to for information about careers in this field?

Employment Interviewing

Finally, take a look at those people/organizations you've identified on your possible-employment-interview list. The purpose of an employment interview is to obtain a position.

If there are people you would like to work for whom you admire and respect, inquire about current or future positions they may have and the possibility of interviewing with them. Or, if there are organizations you would like to work for, research to find a department manager or person who has the authority to hire you and request an employment interview with him/her. Even if there isn't an appropriate open position in that department, ask if you can schedule an appointment anyway. Perhaps a position will be coming open; perhaps the organization will be restructuring; perhaps you will be creating your own position!

It's important for you to know how your skills and accomplishments fit with the person or organization with which you are interviewing. So make sure you've researched the person you'd like to work for and, in the case of an organization, research the values and infrastructure. In either situation, gain as much information as possible so you can show yourself knowledgeable.

To schedule an employment interview, say something like: *"I am very interested in exploring employment with you/your organization and I would like to discuss how my knowledge and skills might compliment your products/services. I would appreciate a few minutes of your time."* If the answer to an interview is yes, schedule it as soon as possible. If the answer to an interview is no, ask if he/she can recommend another individual or organization you might talk to. If the interviewer hesitates or indicates he/she has no current openings, offer to send a resume and references (letters that you have requested from those who know your abilities and work ethics) just in case a position does become available in the future. Be sure to follow up in this situation.

As you probably know, interviews for employment can take many forms. You may be interviewing in front of one interviewer or a panel (several interviewers). Many different kinds of questions may be asked. Some questions may be unrelated to what you have done, but will be asked to gauge your thought processes. If the interviewer has your resume in front of him/her, many of the questions will probably revolve around your accomplishments. The bottom line for any employer, who is genuinely interested in you, is whether he/she can trust you to competently fill a position.

Dress appropriately for the interview and give an energetic first impression by smiling, making eye contact, and giving a firm handshake. In response to questions, steer the answers toward your past performance. Say something like, *"May I share a situation I had in the past...."* The situation you relay may or may not be work-related, but it will demonstrate your abilities. By understanding how you've performed in the past, employers will have a good idea of your future performance in similar situations.

Many times employers will ask if you have any questions for them. Questions you might ask are: *"What might a typical day in this position look like?"* or *"Can you clarify something you mentioned previously?"* or *"Can you shed further light on this part of the position?"*

Also remember, an employment interview is a two-way street. You are determining if this is a person or organization you want to work for. Are you sensing similar values? If so, be persistent in your pursuit and in prayer. Also continue to keep your options open to other possibilities and opportunities; keep an open mind for what God might have for you.

Follow up every interview with a thank-you note. Keep in contact with the interviewer periodically checking your status for a specific or potential position. Make notes on your interview tracking sheet.

Career Guidance

Employment Interview Worksheet

This page is designed to help you prepare for an employment interview.

With whom do you want to schedule an employment interview? _____

What position interests you? _____

What do you know about the position? _____

What are the values of the person/organization? _____

What is the infrastructure of the organization? _____

In addition to accomplishments on your resume, be prepared to give examples of
past performance in areas such as those suggested below. Note: this is not an exhaustive list.

Commitment to task _____

_____

Organization and planning _____

_____

Team orientation _____

_____

Problem-solving ability _____

_____

Multi-tasking _____

_____

Creativity _____

_____

Self-motivation _____

_____

Flexibility _____

_____

As you continue interviewing for similar positions, key themes/similar patterns will emerge
in the interviews, increasing your confidence level. Always remember to pray for wisdom
and guidance before each interview. If you are going through this material with a small group,
practice one-on-one employment interviewing and panel interviewing as well.

Addendum →

The last section of this interactive guide offers additional aids.

<u>In Conclusion:</u>

Interview Tracking Sheet
(Feel free to make copies of this page or transfer the information onto file cards.)

Next Steps
(Feel free to make copies of this page or transfer the information onto file cards.)

Career Change Options

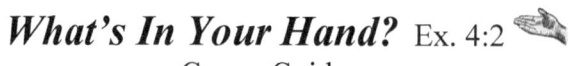
Interview Tracking Sheet

Purpose for Interview: □ **Information**   □ **Employment**
Contact: _____ Date of Interview: _____
Area of Expertise/Position/Title: _____
Organization: _____
Email/Phone #: _____
Referred By: _____
Result of Interview: _____
_____
_____
Date of Thank-You Note: _____
Employment Interview Follow-Up Date and Result: _____
_____

Purpose for Interview: □ **Information**   □ **Employment**
Contact: _____ Date of Interview: _____
Area of Expertise/Position/Title: _____
Organization: _____
Email/Phone #: _____
Referred By: _____
Result of Interview: _____
_____
_____
Date of Thank-You Note: _____
Employment Interview Follow-Up Date and Result: _____
_____

Purpose for Interview: □ **Information**   □ **Employment**
Contact: _____ Date of Interview: _____
Area of Expertise/Position/Title: _____
Organization: _____
Email/Phone #: _____
Referred By: _____
Result of Interview: _____
_____
_____
Date of Thank-You Note: _____
Employment Interview Follow-Up Date and Result: _____
_____

What's In Your Hand? Ex. 4:2
Career Guidance

Next Steps

This page is designed as a planning sheet for you to write down what you see are your next steps in obtaining the career you really want. Consider what research you still need to do, whom you still need to talk to, and where you want to interview.

Research you need to do: How you'll get it done: When you'll get it done:

_____

_____

_____

_____

People you need to talk to: What you need to ask them: When you'll get it done:

_____

_____

_____

_____

Places you want to interview: How you need to proceed: When you'll get it done:

_____

_____

_____

_____

Career Change Options

If you have been re-evaluating your current work situation, this page is designed to help you think about options you may have. Perhaps you feel you've gone as far as you can in your current role. If so, here are a few possibilities to consider.

Let's first consider your current situation.
Where are you now in regard to your career? _____

_____

Would you consider moving across in your organization to another position or department? What would be the benefits? _____

_____

What about growing in place by learning new skills or taking on more responsibility? What would that look like? _____

_____

Could you move up in the organization to a position you are qualified for? What position would interest you? _____

_____

What about moving down either to relieve stress or to regain satisfaction in a prior position? What advantage would this be? _____

_____

On what basis would you consider moving to another organization or becoming entrepreneurial? How would you proceed? _____

_____

Would you consider leaving the field you are currently in and entering a completely new/different field? What would that entail? _____

_____

What's In Your Hand? Ex. 4:2

Career Guidance

Suggested References

<u>What Color Is Your Parachute?</u>
Richard Bolles

Coil & Associates
www.coilscareeradvice.com

John L. Holland
www.self-directed-search.com

Annotation

The first paragraph on page 1 of this packet refers to God having a place and task for all "His children."

According to scripture, only those who take the following steps are considered children of God.

A cknowledge you are a sinner, separated from God, and deserving of punishment.
  Romans 3:23 and Romans 6:23

C onfess your sin to God, repent, and ask forgiveness.
  Romans 10:9-10 and I John 1:9

T rust in Jesus Christ alone to save you.
  John 3:16 and Acts 16:31

Final Thoughts

Now that you have completed this career guide, I hope you have rediscovered what an amazing person you are! You are uniquely and wonderfully designed and I believe God has a specific place for you to serve/witness for Him. In going through this material, I pray you have been encouraged and motivated about the direction of your future. God bless you as you continue to follow God's leading in fulfilling His purpose for your life!

"What's in <u>your</u> hand?"